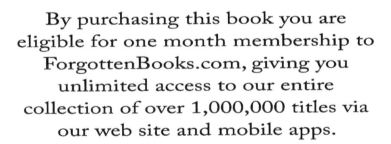

ISBN 978-0-428-79480-4
PIBN 11299545

Canadian Institute for Historical Microreproductions / Institut canadien de microreproductions historiques

Couverture de couleur

☐ Covers damaged /
Couverture endommagée

☐ Covers restored and/or laminated /
Couverture restaurée et/ou pelliculée

☐ Cover title missing / Le titre de couverture manque

☐ Coloured maps / Cartes géographiques en couleur

☐ Coloured ink (i.e. other than blue or black) /
Encre de couleur (i.e. autre que bleue ou noire)

☐ Coloured plates and/or illustrations /
Planches et/ou illustrations en couleur

☐ Bound with other material /
Relié avec d'autres documents

☐ Only edition available /
Seule édition disponible

☐ Tight binding may cause shadows or distortion along
interior margin / La reliure serrée peut causer de
l'ombre ou de la distorsion le long de la marge
intérieure.

☐ Blank leaves added during restorations may appear
within the text. Whenever possible, these have been
omitted from filming / Il se peut que certaines pages
blanches ajoutées lors d'une restauration
apparaissent dans le texte, mais, lorsque cela était
possible, ces pages n'ont pas été filmées.

☐ Pages damaged / Pages endommagées

☐ Pages restored and/or laminated /
Pages restaurées et/ou pelliculées

☑ Pages discoloured, stained or foxed /
Pages décolorées, tachetées ou piquées

☑ Pages detached / Pages détachées

☑ Showthrough / Transparence

☐ Quality of print varies /
Qualité inégale de l'impression

☐ Includes supplementary material /
Comprend du matériel supplémentaire

☐ Pages wholly or partially obscured by errata slips
tissues, etc., have been refilmed to ensure the best
possible image / Les pages totalement ou
partiellement obscurcies par un feuillet d'errata, une
pelure, etc., ont été filmées à nouveau de façon à
obtenir la meilleure image possible.

☐ Opposing pages with varying colouration or
discolourations are filmed twice to ensure the best
possible image / Les pages s'opposent ayant des
colorations variables ou des décolorations sont
filmées deux fois afin d'obtenir la meilleure image
possible.

British Columbia Archives and Records Service.

The images appearing here are the best quality possible considering the condition and legibility of the original copy and in keeping with the filming contract specifications.

Original copies in printed paper covers are filmed beginning with the front cover and ending on the last page with a printed or illustrated impression, or the back cover when appropriate. All other original copies are filmed beginning on the first page with a printed or illustrated impression, and ending on the last page with a printed or illustrated impression.

The last recorded frame on each microfiche shall contain the symbol ➞ (meaning "CONTINUED"), or the symbol ▽ (meaning "END"), whichever applies.

Maps, plates, charts, etc., may be filmed at different reduction ratios. Those too large to be entirely included in one exposure are filmed beginning in the upper left hand corner, left to right and top to bottom, as many frames as required. The following diagrams illustrate the method:

British Columbia Archives and Records Service.

Les images suivantes ont été reproduites avec le plus grand soin, compte tenu de la condition et de la netteté de l'exemplaire filmé, et en conformité avec les conditions du contrat de filmage.

Les exemplaires originaux dont la couverture en papier est imprimée sont filmés en commençant par le premier plat et en terminant soit par la dernière page qui comporte une empreinte d'impression ou d'illustration, soit par le second plat, selon le cas. Tous les autres exemplaires originaux sont filmés en commençant par la première page qui comporte une empreinte d'impression ou d'illustration et en terminant par la dernière page qui comporte une telle empreinte.

Un des symboles suivants apparaîtra sur la dernière image de chaque microfiche, selon le cas: le symbole ➞ signifie "A SUIVRE", le symbole ▽ signifie "FIN".

Les cartes, planches, tableaux, etc., peuvent être filmés à des taux de réduction différents. Lorsque le document est trop grand pour être reproduit en un seul cliché, il est filmé à partir de l'angle supérieur gauche, de gauche à droite, et de haut en bas, en prenant le nombre d'images nécessaire. Les diagrammes suivants illustrent la méthode.

Prospectus——— See Regulations Annexing Table A

The Burleith Mansions,

Limited

Statutory Requirements Attending the Issuance
of this Prospectus

Date of this Prospectus, 10th day of October, 1910.

Signature of Directors at foot.

A copy of this prospectus so signed has been filed for registration.

A copy of the Memorandum complete which is to be read with and form part of this Prospectus is printed at the end hereof, giving signatories and their holding at . . classification of shares.

The Company adopts Table A, which provides that the qualification of a Director shall be the holding of at least **See Regulations Amending Table** one share.

The Directors may not proceed to allotment unless 500 shares are applied for.

The Vendor of the property is Dr. Frank Hall. The consideration to be paid him is $26,000.

Ten per cent. cash is to be paid as commission for subscribing or agreeing to subscribe to the debentures and shares respectively.

The preliminary expense is estimated at $1,500.

There is no consideration to the promoter, and there is no material contract.

W. Curtis Sampson, Victoria, B.C., is the Auditor of the Company appointed until the annual meeting in the year 1911.

The Directors have no interest in the promotion of or in the property proposed to be acquired by the Company.

The right of voting at meetings of the Company is, a vote a share.

The statements herein set forth are based on information furnished by Messrs. Bond & Clark, but applicants will be deemed to agree with the Company (as Trustees for the Directors) that they will not make any claim under Sections 89, 90 and 92 of the Companies' Act on account of any incorrect statement in the Prospectus made by any Director in the belief that it was correct or claim to repudiate their contract on that account.

The Following is the Opinion of an Expert

———

Messrs. Bond & Clark,
      Victoria, B.C.

Victoria, B.C., August 25th, 1910.

Dear Sirs:—

As per instructions received from you we have inspected Burleith Lodge and the property that belongs to same, viz.: 22 lots.

This house was formerly owned by Mr. James Dunsmuir as a residence and was sold by auction recently by a syndicate who had acquired this and adjoining property, to Dr. Frank Hall for the sum of $21,000. He has since spent on the property between $3,000 and $4,000, and as you state has now given you an option on the property for 60 days from this date at $26,000.

Our valuation of the property is as follows:

Two waterfront lots fronting on Victoria Arm, $2,500 each, $5,000; 20 inside lots of an average valuation of $600 each, $12,000. We have our valuation of this property on the fact that we have sold and owned nearly 100 lots in this vicinity and have sold within the past week inside lots on McPherson Avenue, an adjoining street in a locality not quite as good, for $1,000 each. We also owned and sold the adjoining waterfront property to Burleith consisting of about 4 acres.

The House—The building originally cost, we are informed by the people who are in a position to know, $70,000, and the house is in a good state of repair and magnificently finished. We would consider the house worth as a Hotel and Boarding House proposition at least $30,000; any necessary changes can be done at a moderate cost.

Taken as a whole, however, we would consider that the proposition is worth more money as the situation for a high class hotel and boarding house is ideal. The Oak Bay Hotel is the only place of a similar character in the vicinity of the City and it is so crowded at all times that people have to book at least two months ahead to get accommodation. The boating and bathing at Burleith is the finest on the Coast as the water is protected and safe and the water is warm, as the tide runs in so far before it gets there.

It is conveniently situated in the centre of the City, the Gorge car running past the property via the Craigflower Road, which is the main thoroughfare from the rural districts of Metchosin, Goldstream, etc.

If this place is run on a proper plan, we think it can be filled with a high class trade the year round.

Yours respectfully,

H. M. FULLERTON.

Summary		
2 Waterfront Lots	$ 5,000
20 Inside Lots	12,000
Building	30,000
	$47,000

Fleming

"BURLEITH," FRONT VIEW

Fleming Bros., 1905

HALL AND STAIRWAY, FINISHED IN OAK, BEAUTIFULLY CARVED

Fleming Bros., 1905

ASSEMBLY HALL, GUESTS AND BOARDERS RENDEZVOUS

Fleming Bros., 1905

GUESTS RECEPTION ROOM, MANTEL, COSY CORNER, AND ROOM THROUGHOUT FINISHED IN BIRDSEYE MAPLE

Corner View of Amusement and Recreation Room

Crocker, 1905

TERRACE IN FRONT OF MUSIC ROOM

Crocker, 1905

FLOWER GARDENS BELOW MUSIC ROOM

Drive and View of Grounds from West Side

THE "COMPANIES ACT"

MEMORANDUM OF ASSOCIATION

of the

Burleith Mansions,

Limited

1. The name of the Company is "Burleith Mansions, Limited."

2. The Registered Office of the Company will be in the City of Victoria, Province of British Columbia.

3. The objects for which the Company is established are:—

(1) To purchase of Dr. Frank Hall the residence and adjacent area consisting of five acres more or less of Mr. James Dunsmuir acquired by Dr. Frank Hall, and now under option of sale dated the 24th day of August, 1910, to Messrs. Bond & Clark, Trustees for this Company, and to carry into effect the said agreement.

(2) To reconstruct, remodel, enlarge, alter and construct additional buildings upon the said area and to furnish and equip the same;

(3) To carry on the business of a private unlicensed hotel with board and lodging accommodation and all other accommodation usually given in unlicensed hotels, boarding houses and restaurants, and to carry on with such business the business of a bathing establishment with laundries, dressing-rooms, reading, writing and newspaper rooms, libraries, grounds and other places of amusement, recreation, sport, entertainment and instruction of all kinds;

(4) To establish, maintain and conduct an unlicensed Club of a non-political character (unlicensed for the sale of liquor) for the accommodation of members of the Company and their friends, and to use and operate the buildings of the Company as and for a Club House and other convenience and generally to afford to members and their friends all the usual privileges, advantages and conveniences of accommodation of a Club;

(5) To carry on any other business which may seem to the Company capable of being conveniently carried on in connection with the above or calculated directly or indirectly to enhance the value of and to render profitable any of the Company's property or rights;

(6) To acquire and undertake the whole or any p   ' the business, property and liabilities of any person or Company carrying on any business which the Company is aut   d to carry on, or possessed of property suitable for the purposes of this Company;

(7) To enter into any arrangements with any Municipal, local or other authority that may seem conducive to the Company's objects or any of them, and to obtain from any such authority any rights, privileges and concessions which the Company may think it desirable to obtain, and to carry out, exercise and comply with any such arrangements, rights, privileges and concessions;

(8) Generally to purchase, take on lease or in exchange, or otherwise acquire any real and personal property, and any rights or privileges which the Company may think necessary or convenient for the purposes of its business, and to construct, maintain and alter any buildings, erections, garden or ground embellishment and plantings, or works necessary or convenient for the purposes of the Company;

(9) To invest and deal with the moneys of the Company not immediately required in such manner as from time to time may be determined;

(10) To lend money to such persons and on such terms as may seem expedient and particularly to customers and others having dealings with the Company, and to guarantee the performance of contracts by any such persons;

(11) To borrow or raise money for any purpose of the Company and to secure the payment of same and interest in such manner as the Company shall think fit, and in particular by the issue of debentures or debenture stock perpetual or otherwise charged upon all or any of the Company's property, both present and future, including its uncalled capital and to purchase, redeem or pay for any such securities;

(12) To remunerate any person or Company for services rendered or to be rendered in placing or assisting to place, or guaranteeing the placing of any of the shares of the Company's capital, or any debenture, debenture stock or other securities of the Company, or in or about the formation or promotion of the Company or conduct of its business;

(13) To draw, make, accept, endorse, discount, execute and issue promissory notes, bills of exchange, bills of lading, warrants, debentures and other negotiable or transferable instruments;

(14) To adopt such means of making known the operations of the Company as may seem expedient; and in particular by advertising in the Press, by circulars, by purchase and exhibition of works of art or interest, by publication of books and periodicals, and by granting prizes, rewards and donations;

(15) To sell, improve, manage, develop, exchange, lease, mortgage, dispose of, turn to account or otherwise deal with all or any part of the property and rights of the Company;

(16) To do all or any of the above things as principals, agents, directors, trustees or otherwise, and by or through trustees, agents or otherwise, and either alone or in conjunction with the others;

(17) To do all such other things as are incidental or conducive to the attainment of the above objects;

(18) To accumulate funds and to admit any person or persons to participate in the profits or assets of the Company;

(19) To distribute any of the assets for the time being of the Company among the members in kind, and to stipulate for and obtain for the members or any of them any of the rights, privileges or options;

(20) To acquire by surrender or otherwise the whole or any part of the interest of any member of the Company therein;

(21) To assign to any member or class of member any preferential, special or qualified rights or privileges over or as compared with any other members as regards participation in profits or assets and as regards voting and as regards winding up, or otherwise howsoever;

(22) To purchase or otherwise acquire on such terms or in such manner as the regulations of the Company from time to time provide in shares in the Company's capital;

(23) To distribute any of the property of the Company in specie among the members.

4. The liability of the members is limited.

5. The share capital of the Company is One hundred thousand dollars, divided into ten thousand shares of ten dollars each.

Any of the shares in the capital, original or increased, may be issued with any preferential, special or qualified rights or conditions as regards dividends, capital, voting or otherwise attached thereto.

We, the several persons whose names and addresses are subscribed hereto, are desirous of being formed into a Company in pursuance of this Memorandum of Association, and we respectively agree to take the number of shares in the capital set opposite our respective names.

NAMES, ADDRESSES AND DESCRIPTION OF SUBSCRIBERS	No. of Shares Taken
HONOURABLE EDGAR DEWDNEY, Victoria, B. C., Civil Engineer.	ONE
ERNEST AMOS HALL, 725 Fort Street, Victoria, B. C., Physician.	ONE
WILLIAM ANGUS GLEASON, 1452 Vining Street, Victoria, B. C., Contractor.	ONE
ANGUS BEATON McNEILL, 622 Trounce Avenue, Victoria, B. C., Real Estate Agent.	ONE
ALEXANDER PEDEN, 611 Fort Street, Victoria, B. C., Merchant.	ONE

Dated this 30th day of September, 1910.

Witness to all the above signatures:

C. DUBOIS MASON,
Victoria, B. C.,
Solicitor.

ADDITIONS -to- "DURLEITH"

— Scale 8 feet to 1 inch —

— All new finish to match that on existing building as far as possible —

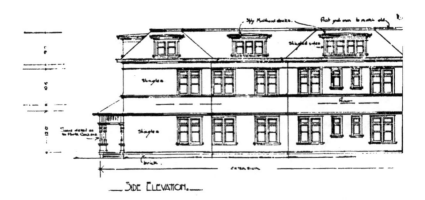

SIDE ELEVATION.

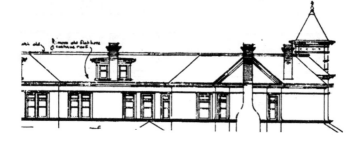

ADDITIONS & DWELLING VICTOR

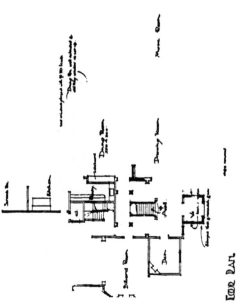

FLOOR PLAN.

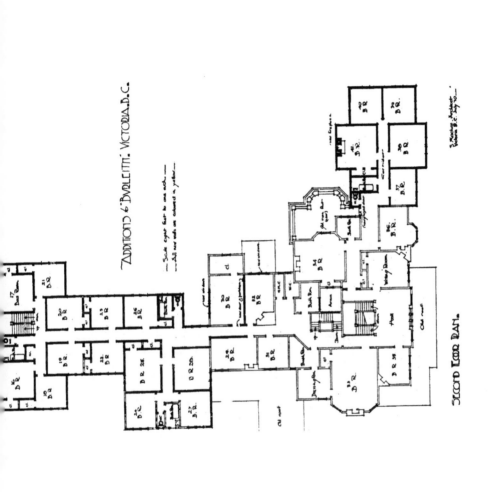

ADDITIONS &'BURLEITH'. VICTORIA. B.C.

—Scale eight feet to one inch.—
—All new work an coloured in yellow.—

SECOND FLOOR PLAN.

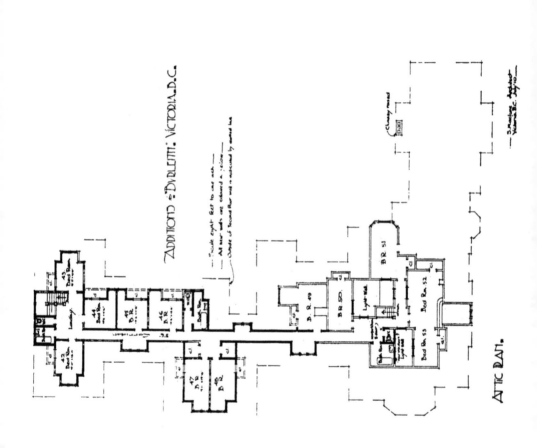

ADDITIONS to DUNLEITH. VICTORIA, D.C.

Scale eight feet to one inch
All new work not coloured a yellow
Outside of Second Floor wall is indicated by dotted line

S. Maclure, Architect
Victoria, B.C. 1910

ATTIC PLAN.

The "Companies' Act"

Burleith Mansions, Limited

CAPITAL $100,000.00

Issue of $100,000 in 10,000 $10.00 shares, payable $2.00 per share on application, $2.00 on allotment, the balance at call in amounts not exceeding $2.00, but so that two months must elapse between each call.

DIRECTORS

HONOURABLE EDGAR DEWDNEY,
Victoria, B. C.,
Civil Engineer.

WILLIAM ANGUS GLEASON,
1452 Vining Street,
Victoria, B. C.,
Contractor.

ERNEST AMOS HALL,
725 Fort Street,
Victoria, B. C.,
Physician.

ANGUS BEATON McNEILL,
622 Trounce Avenue,
Victoria, B. C.,
Real Estate Agent.

ALEXANDER PEDEN,
611 Fort Street,
Victoria, B. C.,
Merchant.

SECRETARY, EDWIN COVENTRY, Esq., Victoria, B.C.

SOLICITORS, MASON & MANN, VICTORIA, B.C.

ARCHITECT, S. MACLURE, Esq.

AUDITOR, W. CURTIS SAMPSON, Esq., VICTORIA, B.C.   BANKERS, THE MERCHANTS BANK OF CANADA, VICTORIA, B. C.

As will be seen by the annexed printed report, which is to be taken as part of this Prospectus, it has been estimated that there exists a profitable business enterprise in acquiring the late residence of Mr. James Dunsmuir standing on about five acres of land with water frontage on Victoria Arm, and converting the same to provide suitable accommodation for guests and to operate a private unlicensed hotel to be conducted on the lines of a private unlicensed hotel or restaurant combined with some of the advantages of a private Club. This will be effected by inducing resident customers to take shares and become co-proprietors.

There is upon the property an existing encumbrance of $10,000. It is intended by means of 8 per cent. debentures to seek to raise the sum of $50,000 thereout to pay the incumbrance aforesaid, the price to Dr. Hall and, with the assistance of share capital, the cost of additions and furnishings.

The debentures are in amounts of $100 and will be issued by the Company as a charge upon the whole of its unincumbered real and personal property including its uncalled capital. The debentures will share equally and carry interest at 8 per cent. per annum and can be paid off at any time by one month's notice by the Company, or will be paid out by the Company on twelve months' notice. Interest payable half yearly. It is of course intended to discharge these debentures numerically as soon as possible.

The Following is the Option

Messrs. Bond & Clark,   Victoria, B.C., August 24th, 1910
    on behalf of
        The Burleith Mansions, Ltd.

Gentlemen:—

In consideration of one dollar now paid to me, I hereby give you until the 1st day of November, 1910, at 5 o'clock in the afternoon to elect in writing to purchase from me the property recently acquired by me at auction known as Burleith Lodge, Victoria West, lately the residence of Mr. James Dunsmuir, with the grounds consisting of five acres, more or less, for the sum of $26,000, which may be paid as follows:—$10,000 is now owing on agreement of sale on the property which has about one and onehalf years to run; this may remain for this time, or be paid off at your expense. The balance of $16,000 to be paid to me as follows: $6,000 on the first day of November, 1910, and the balance of $10,000 on the first day of November, 1911, with interest at 6 per cent. per annum from the date of giving possession of the property.

I am willing to give possession wh . the $6,000 is paid and mortgage for $10,000 is executed, you to give me two to four weeks' notice to vacate.

                          Yours faithfully,
                          FRANK HALL, M.D.

CPSIA information can be obtained
at www.ICGtesting.com
Printed in the USA
BVHW090721081118

532427BV00011B/635/P